QUOTATIONS FROM
CHAIRMAN CHERRY

QUOTATIONS FROM CHAIRMAN CHERRY

Compiled, Annotated
& Introduced by

ALLAN SAFARIK
& DOLORES REIMER

A LITTLE RED BOOK
ARSENAL PULP PRESS

A LITTLE RED BOOK

QUOTATIONS FROM CHAIRMAN
CHERRY

ISBN 0-88978-236-9

CIP DATA: SEE PAGE 6

LITTLE RED BOOKS ARE
PUBLISHED BY
ARSENAL PULP PRESS
1062 HOMER STREET #100
VANCOUVER BC V6B 2W9
Cover: Kelly Brooks
Illustration: Kirk Lawton
Typesetting: Vancouver Desktop
Publishing Centre
Printing: Webcom
Printed and bound in Canada

CONTENTS

ACKNOWLEDGEMENT

Thanks to Scott Kusalik and Jim Mullin
for additional material.

CANADIAN CATALOGUING
IN PUBLICATION DATA

Cherry, Don, 1934-
    Quotations from chairman Cherry
    (A Little red book)
    Includes bibliographical references
and index.
    ISBN 0-88978-236-9
    1. Cherry, Don, 1934-   —Quotations.
2. Hockey—Coaches—Quotations. 3.
Sportscasters—Canada—Quotations.
I. Safarik, Allan, 1948-   II. title.
III. Series.
GV848.5.C54A3 1992   796.962'092
C92-091713-5

INTRODUCTION

It has been said that hockey in Canada is a religion; certainly its devotees are legion and its practitioners tenacious in their pursuit of its goals. But every religion needs its mullahs, its archbishops, its popes, its Chairmen, if you will; and it is only during the current epoch that we have seen rise among us such a leader—in the evanescent, slightly fluorescent figure of Chairman Cherry, whose three-minute homilies on the enigma of hockey have enlightened much of the nation.

We hope the deeper mysteries of Cherry Thought will be illu-

minated in this compilation of
homily, adage, gospel and wild
remark. Cherry Thought is not, of
course, for the timidly-minded.
Whether the subject be Swedes,
Soviets, high collars or natty
suits, Chairman Cherry is not one
to mince his own words. Chairman Cherry is first of all a survi-
vor; his career is an arc rising
from Springfield to Hershey by
way of Trois Rivières, Sudbury
and Spokane, to the glory of Boston and the ignominy of Denver.
Never a man to fall back on job
security, but always with a good
word for his canine companion,
Chairman Cherry is the national
conduit of rink-lore, ever-mind-

ful of the virtues of the past and the vices of the present.

ON BECOMING ONESELF:
THE PRE-REQUISITES

It isn't easy to become Don Cherry. For starters, you need to have a mother named Maude and a father named Delmar.

ON INHERITING A SARTORIAL
VISION FROM ONE'S FATHER

I have a vision of him standing on the corner in front of Pappa's Pool Hall wearing a black homburg hat, tailor made suit, tight-fitting vest, and diamond stick pin glistening in the sun.

ON THE LESSONS OF MEMORY

Never forget a friend, and never forget an enemy.

ON DEVELOPING AN EARLY AMBITION FOR SETTING RECORDS

I set the record—unofficially of course—for being strapped by the principal of Rideau Elementary School.

ON GETTING AT LEAST ONE THING RIGHT

The only thing I managed to get right in school was the notation in my year book: "Ambition—pro hockey player."

ON THAT ONE THING HAVING TO BE GOOD ENOUGH

For me arithmetic was as easy as

doping out Einstein's Theory of Relativity.

ON MAKING A PERFECT COUPLE

I was a big, hotheaded, belligerent, Scots-Irish Protestant attracted to a tiny, frail, quiet, Italian Catholic. We had nothing whatsoever in common.

ONE WAY TO IMPRESS THE FUTURE IN-LAWS

I was beautiful. I had stitches on my forehead, my eyes were a mess. What an impression.

ONE WAY TO IMPRESS
THE HAPPY BRIDE

We spent our honeymoon in Miami Beach during a hurricane.

ON THE CANINE POWER BEHIND
THE THRONE

Blue has been the real brains behind my success.

ON DOING ONE'S BIT
WHEREVER ONE CAN

My contribution to hockey was figuring out how to keep the beer cold during a long bus trip. I think I was the first guy to put beer in a pillow case and hang it out the bus window. Also I taught the guys how to open

them without the coach hearing.
That was big too.

ON MAKING
A SARTORIAL IMPRESSION

Even then, I had the best suits and
best shirts. I always looked sharp.
The kids didn't have shoes, but I
always looked good.

A LASTING MEMORY
OF SUDBURY, ONTARIO

It was so cold down there you
had to take a blanket with you
whenever you went to the toilet.

ON EARNING A MONIKER FROM
EDDIE SHORE

He gave me a nickname—The

Madagascar Kid. I think that's where he would have sent me, given the opportunity.

ON GETTING TO
TROIS RIVIERES, ACCORDING
TO EDDIE SHORE

Nothing to it, 'Madagascar.' You go up through New Hampshire; then over to Vermont and when you hit the Canadian border, turn right.

EDDIE SHORE
IN A NUTSHELL

The Darth Vader of hockey.

EDDIE SHORE'S
TERPSICHOREAN SECRET

He opened training camp by having his players tap dance and then execute ballet steps on the ice.

ON WHAT IT MEANT TO GET ON
EDDIE'S SHIT LIST

The Black Aces were required to do odd jobs around the arena such as painting seats, selling programs, making popcorn, and blowing up hundreds of balloons.

ON THE INTELLECTUAL LIFE
OF EDDIE SHORE

He had more theories than there

are pucks in the world. The man sent shivers up a player's spine.

ON THE IMPORTANCE OF SELF-KNOWLEDGE, ESPECIALLY IN EDDIE'S CASE

Some people are nuts and never realize it. At least Eddie had an inkling.

ON LARRY ZIEDAL AND THE SALUBRIOUS EFFECTS OF THE PHONOGRAPH

He used to play John Philip Sousa marches on the phonograph in the afternoon so that by nightfall he was ready to tramp onto the ice and mow down anybody in sight.

ON LARRY ZIEDAL AND THE
STATE OF ONE'S DENTITION

Those who ran afoul of my partner Larry Ziedal certainly didn't
have their own teeth.

ON ACHIEVING THE SUBLIME
WITH THE SUCKER PUNCH

I became so proficient at it I could
sucker a guy sleeping on a bed.

ON ZIEDALISM AND
PSYCHING THEM OUT

The opposition used to think he
was crazy hearing him shout "X-
Y" or "X-C" (a couple of our secret plays) during one of our
counter-attacks.

ON REVENGE IN THE
ZIEDALIST MODE

Larry drew back his stick like a hypnotist and drove it right up [Bo] Elik's nose.

ON DEFENDING
ZIEDALISM

Larry didn't deserve that misconduct. Stewart turned to me and there was a big hunk of spit rolling right down his eye.

ON THE AMBIGUOUS BENEFITS
OF PLAYING FOR
THE SPOKANE COMETS

My partner turned out to be a mean cuss named Cornelius Patrick Madigan, alias the Mad Dog.

ON KEEPING UP MORALE,
MAD DOG STYLE

He used to beat up his own teammates before the team picture.

ON GETTING THE RIGHT PRICE

I became a Canadien for two rolls
of tape and a jock strap.

ON THE EFFECTS
OF THINKING

In the minors you never thought.
If you ever thought—no educa-
tion, no trade, you're playing
hockey—where are you going in
the minors? You had fun and you
played.

A THOUGHT TO KEEP ON GOING BY

I thought I was gonna play forever. I never thought it would end.

ON STRAIGHT TALK IN A NAUTICAL MODE

I used to tell the guys at training camp, "We're going on a long voyage. Some of you will make it; others are going over the side."

ON WHAT BOSTON MISSED

When I went to Boston, I took over the whole city. I was unbelievable. I could have run for mayor.

ON WHAT LIFE IN BOSTON
CAN DO

Some of the players were fat, and not only physically, but fat in the heart.

BOBBY ORR IN A NUTSHELL

He was the greatest hockey player I have ever seen, Gordie Howe and Wayne Gretzky included.

ON THE SECRET BEHIND THE
BEST HOCKEY PLAYER
IN THE WORLD

Well, the best hockey player in the world, as far as anybody says, is Bobby Orr—that ever was or ever has been ... But you take the last year that I coached him, he had forty-six goals, eighty-three assists and he was plus 128, which is, you know . . . nobody seems to come close to that.

ON THE EQUESTRIAN TRUTH ABOUT BOBBY ORR

I learned early just to let him play his own game; you don't pull the reins on Secretariat.

ON BOBBY ORR AND THE BOSTON ANALOGUE

A Boston institution just like Bunker Hill.

ON HECKLERS IN BOSTON

The crowd disliked Don Mc-

Kenny and Ken Hodge and used to call them 'Mary' because they weren't tough enough.

We're the Boston Bruins; we don't worry about any other team, they worry about us.

He loved his hair . . . . After a game he would sit in his brown and white kimono, apply a white solution to his hair, and then sit with the conditioner settling in to make it even more beautiful.

ON UNPLEASANT SIDE EFFECTS
OF ESPOSITO'S COIFFURE

I remember one night we were playing a crucial game at Boston Gardens and as I patrolled the area behind the bench I noticed the back of Phil's neck. " Phil," I said, " you look like you're oozing dark blood." He felt the back of his head, looked at his palm and said; "Grapes, I'm gonna kill that hairdresser."

REMARKS ON MEETING STAN
JONATHAN'S FATHER

You've got a great son there, Mr. Jonathan. He reminds me of my dog Blue.

ON GREAT COMMANDERS
IN HISTORY

For my money there was only one role in history that could surpass running the Bruins and that would be being Lord Nelson commanding the fleet at Trafalgar. He was killed in that action too.

ON VIEWING ADMIRAL
NELSON'S WAISTCOAT AND
MEDALS AT THE BRITISH
MUSEUM

I was just in awe, I couldn't believe no one else was looking at it.

ON BEING PREPARED TO BREAK
OUT THE CAT O'NINE TAILS

Nelson, you know, would've done anything for his men, and that's what I did when I coached. I would have done anything for my players. I treated them like the crew of the ship.

ON EARLY INFLUENCES AND
THE HISTORY OF
THE BRITISH EMPIRE

Now Drake and Nelson, they knew how to handle men, the whole deal and they were always in trouble with their bosses too. I must've read every book about them when I was a kid and I don't know whether that shaped me to always be against my bosses, which is bad, I guess, because you're never going to win if you're against your bosses.

ON BEING PREPARED TO DO ANYTHING FOR JOHN WENSINK

His skating was so atrocious I had half a mind to buy him a pair of double runners.

ON BEING PREPARED FOR PLAYERS WHO GET DRUNK ON AIRPLANES

I flew out of my chair, grabbed him by the throat and sunk my fingernails into his Adam's apple.

ON THE SPECIAL TALENTS OF
BOBBY SCHMAUTZ

The enemy called him "the surgeon" and not because he was genteel with his scalpel.

ON BOBBY SCHMAUTZ AND
THE YULETIDE SPIRIT

We used to say that at Christmas, instead of using a knife, Schmautzie carved the turkey with his hockey stick.

ON THE IMPLICATIONS OF
MIKE MILBURY'S SOFT SPOT

You happy pacifist, you'll never make the big time.

ON WHAT TERRY O'REILLY'S TRAGIC FLAW WOULD BE, IF HE WERE TO HAVE ONE

If he had one flaw it was a vicious temper.

ON THE PRICE OF COUNTENANCING JEAN RATELLE

I felt as if I were confronting the parish priest.

ON THE ROLE OF SIDEKICK BLUE IN FINDING GOALIES

Blue picks them for me. We go for walks and she picks which goalie is going to be hot.

ON THE DARKER SIDE OF THE
CURATORIAL PROFESSION

Working with Orr was for me like being a museum curator, watching an extremely valuable piece of art disintegrate before your eyes.

ON WHAT THEY LEFT IN
IN BRAD PARK

His knees had all the cartilages taken out but they never took his heart out.

ON THE PRICE OF SARTORIAL
SHARPNESS IN BOSTON

In Boston I had suits that were so tight I couldn't sit down. They were really sharp.

ON WHAT YOU CAN'T TAKE OUT OF QUEBECERS

French Canadian players have a special pride in their culture. Playing in the Montreal Forum is to them what a pilgrimage to Mecca is to a Moslem.

ON THE IMMENSITY OF EVEN THINKING ABOUT STOPPING GUY LAFLEUR

Sounds easy. About as easy as bottling the Atlantic Ocean.

ON THE PRICE OF GETTING INTO OVERTIME IN THE STANLEY CUP FINALS

Park, Schmautz and Cashman

had blood running into their un-
derwear.

ON THE INFAMOUS
TOO-MEN-ON-THE ICE
PENALTY THAT COST THE
BRUINS THE STANLEY CUP IN
1972

I needed a large—about a 40 foot
long—invisible hook to instantly
haul in my wandering minstrel.

ON WHO PUT THAT WANDERING
MINSTREL THERE IN
THE FIRST PLACE

Sometimes when you have too
many men on the ice it's the
players' fault. But not this time.

ON THE MONTREAL CANADIENS
AND WHAT'S RED
IN TOOTH AND CLAW

They looked like a pride of lions
about to jump a wildebeast.

FURTHER IMPLICATIONS OF
THINKING ABOUT STOPPING
GUY LAFLEUR

Lafleur was moving down the ice
like the Japanese Bullet Train.

ON THE PRICE OF WANTING TO
CONTINUE TO LIVE
WITH ONESELF

If I had to kiss someone's ass to
keep my job, I couldn't live with
myself.

ON GETTING THINGS INTO AN HISTORICAL PERSPECTIVE

There were Frick and Frack, Hope and Crosby, and finally, Cherry and Sinden [Bruin's GM].

ON THE INEXORABLE EVOLUTION OF THE CHERRY-SINDEN PARTNERSHIP

We had grown farther apart than the Hatfields and McCoys.

ON THE PRICE ONE OUGHT TO PAY

I didn't need anyone telling me how to coach or who to play. I spent 23 years riding the busses. I paid my dues.

ON THE DEVOLVING
MUTUALITY OF THE
CHERRY-SINDEN RELATIONSHIP

I can guarantee I liked him more than he liked me.

ON HARRY SINDEN'S
SOFT SPOT

He put together the Big Bad Bruins and won two Stanley Cups. But if you ever saw Harry Sinden play you'd know why he doesn't like fighting.

ON HAVING A LOT OF FUN
WITH HARRY SINDEN

I don't know what I'd do without Harry. I have a lot of fun with him. Like, he said he was going to

poke me in the nose and I said
he'd have to get a stool to reach
my nose. Heh, heh.

ON THE IMPLICATIONS OF WORKING FOR HAROLD BALLARD

I'm too much like him. One of us
would end up dead—and know-
ing his record, it would be me.

ON THE MORBID SIDE OF THE IMPLICATIONS OF WORKING FOR RAY MIRON AND THE COLORADO ROCKIES

The more I got my name in the
paper the more I realized I was
digging my own grave.

ON FIGHTING BOTH ENDS
AGAINST THE MIDDLE WITH
THE COLORADO ROCKIES

My best drinker couldn't drink and my best goal scorer was the best drinker.

ON WHAT
THE PEOPLE WANT

You have to give people something else besides a win. People have to have fun. In Colorado we only had nineteen wins, but we drew 153,000 more people than the previous year.

ON THE TROUBLE WITH THE
COLORADO ROCKIES

I needed a team of Lord Fauntelroys like a moose needs a hat rack.

ON WHAT IT MEANS TO HAVE A FEW REAL ONES ON ONE'S TEAM

Even a poultry expert wouldn't buy some of the turkeys we had on our roster.

ON THE SIGNIFICANCE OF MERLIN MALINOSKI'S *MAGICIAN* MONIKER

Anyone who could stay in the NHL with his talent had to be a magician.

ON WHERE TO LOOK FOR MIKE MCEWAN

His teammates called him Space

Cadet because he often behaved as if he had a condominium somewhere between Venus and Mars.

ON HOW TO SPOT THE GUYS WHO PLAY HOCKEY OR WHATEVER

The guys that drink beer are the guys who play hockey or slow-pitch, not the tennis players or the golfers who are drinking Pear-i-air water.

ON CLASS STRUGGLE AND THE HOCKEY WORLD

Those guys that score goals, lots of goals, they're the ones driving Cadillacs! Those guys that pass the puck to let them score the goals, they're the guys that drive Volkswagons.

ON WAYNE GRETZKY'S CAMPAIGN TO CURTAIL FIGHTING IN THE NHL

It really upsets him that his friends in L.A. see a baseball brawl, and they say, 'Look it's a hockey game.' Well I'm sorry, but I don't care what Arsenio Hall thinks.

ON ONE THING THAT'S WRONG WITH WAYNE GRETZKY

He has become the social conscience of hockey.

ON WHAT'S HAPPENING IN HOCKEY EVEN TO THE OLD GUYS

Drugs are not a problem and players drink only half as much as they used to. Hell you can't even get an old guy to go out for a beer anymore.

ON IRONY AND THE NEW BARBARISM

I know it sounds barbaric, but in college hockey, and other U.S. hockey, sticking has gone up. There's the old story, if you stick me and I can't drop my gloves, I'm going to stick you back with my stick. For sure, somehow or other, they've got to get the high sticking out. Last year everybody was thrilled that there were only eight fights in the whole playoffs but they failed to realize that there were twenty sticking majors. That means that twenty guys were cut that they caught. I mean, you wouldn't get twenty guys cut in a whole season a few years ago. So the sticks are up and it's too bad. We just have to do something.

ON THE PERFECT DATE

A few pops, a sauna, and the salmon and cheese sandwiches my wife Rose always packs for me. Love 'em. I'm still a minor leaguer at heart.

ON WHAT'S WRONG WITH
EUROPEAN HOCKEY PLAYERS

It's just a job with Europeans.
They lack intensity. Our playoffs
don't excite them. They just want
to get home.

ON ALPO SUHONEN'S
APPOINTMENT AS ASSISTANT
COACH FOR THE WINNIPEG JETS

Alpo is a dog food, isn't it?

ON ANY SECOND THOUGHTS
BARRY SHENKAROW MIGHT
HAVE ABOUT ONE'S THOUGHTS
ON ALPO SUHONEN'S NAME

Look, Alpo is the name of a dog
food, isn't it? Sure I made fun of
his name but he didn't take of-

fence to it. And he calls me a racist. Who maligned who here?

ON HAVING A PICTURE OF FORMER ISLANDER STEFAN PERSSON, BATTERED AND BLEEDING, ON THE WALL OF ONE'S RESTAURANT

I had to have a picture of a bleeding Swede.

ON THE LUNCH-MEAT FLAWS OF MULTI-CULTURALISM

This cultural mosaic stuff is a bunch of baloney . . . I'm Scotch, and I've got a kilt, but I don't demand that anybody puts up with my kilt. The only reason a lot of these people left their country was because they couldn't make a go of it. Then, the first thing they try to do is change Canada into the country they left.

ON IMMIGRANTS WHO WORK THE GRAVEYARD SHIFT

When I come into an airport at 2 a.m., guess who takes my ticket? They work hard, and they're all right in my book.

ON LEAVING THE ANGLICANS FOR THE PRESBYTERIANS

They were getting too left wing .... I'm not going to sit there every Sunday and listen to somebody I don't agree with.

ON DEFENDING THE CANADIAN JUNIORS FOR BRAWLING WITH THE SOVIETS AT THE 1987 WORLD CHAMPIONSHIP

I said to myself 'Boy oh boy, you could be finished forever on television. All you have to say is isn't this terrible and this shouldn't happen and get out of there.' But I said to hell with it. The left-wing pinkos were ripping me to shreds but it was 20 Russians and 5 Canadians.

ON THE ENGLISH LANGUAGE AND THE LANGUAGE POLICE

Some people in CBC said they owed it to the English-speaking children of Canada to have me put off the air. They said I was destroying the English Language.

ON KNOWING WHO YOU'RE TALKING TO

There's a lot of mothers that don't like it, there's a lot of college professors that don't like it. But I'm talking to the guy that goes in the beverage halls.

ON THINKING ABOUT WHAT OTHER PEOPLE THINK ABOUT ONE

I'm just me. I'm like bagpipes— either you like them or you hate them.

ON ONE'S LIFE:
THE ACROBATIC ANALOGUE

I walked a tightrope as a coach and I walk a tightrope on TV.

ON KNOWING WHICH WAY
THE WIND BLOWS

If my wife tells me they [the CBC] haven't phoned by Friday, I know I'm still working on Saturday.

ON DEVELOPING A SENSE OF
CLASS SOLIDARITY

Every time I drive by those guys that are workin' on the highway with a jackhammer, I have a guilty feeling that I should be there too.

ON HOW STIFF COLLARS ARE SO MUCH LIKE OTHER THINGS IN LIFE

You have to get used to them.

ON WHAT TO THINK WHEN, OILER DEFENSEMAN AND ERSTWHILE PHYSICIAN RANDY GREGG MISSES AN OPEN NET

How would you like that guy operating on you with those hands?

ON TAKING UMBRAGE AT BEING STOPPED BY A MOTORCYCLE POLICEMAN

He was wearing a visor. I thought he was a Russian.

ON THE ENDLESS JOKES
OF RON MACLEAN

A million comedians starving to death and you're trying to be one.

ON RON MACLEAN'S
CRITICISM OF ONE'S COACHING

Yeah, well what can you expect from a guy who refs in his spare time.

ON FANS:
HOW TO SEPARATE
THE SHEEP FROM
THE GOATS

The fans that pay the money are the ones that seem to like the fighting. The people that don't seem to like the fighting are the ones who get in free like the press and Harry Sinden.

ON THE BOSTON BRUINS AND THE POWER OF NOSTALGIA

I love them so much I still wear their shorts.

ON BEING PREPARED FOR THE AXE TO DROP

I'm just glad I've got those restaurants because the way I act I could be gone anytime.

ON ACTING A CERTAIN AGE

I still act like I'm 38.

ON WHAT NOT EVERYONE
CAN SAY

I've been paid by hockey since I was 16.

ON THE PRICE OF
MAINTAINING ONE'S
INTEGRITY ON TV

I think I'll last a couple more years . . . . I love doing it, the reason is because I don't have to compromise. If I thought I had to compromise I wouldn't do it.

ON SURVIVAL
IN THE WASTELAND
OF TELEVISION

The secret is to leave them wanting more, so they are going to be

tuned in next week. My first pro-
ducer told me that was the way to
survive in this business.

ON THE PLACE OF ELOCUTION IN KNOWING WHO YOU'RE TALKING TO

People like me because I pro-
nounce the names like the aver-
age working guy when I do
television.

ON CALLING CRITICS OF CANADA IN THE GULF WAR *KOOKS* ON TELEVISION

It had to be done, and where else
was I going to do it?

Mankind? I don't know if those guys in Africa give a darn.

No. 1, the Zamboni driver; No. 2, an usher; No. 3, a guy selling popcorn.

I'm not a diplomat. I still think I talk like a coach.

ON HOW OLD HOCKEY FANS
TEND MERELY TO FADE AWAY

I'm like an old horse trader who never gets tired of the track. I watch the Streetsville minor team on the cable station here when there's nothing else on.

ON LIFE,
WITH A SECOND THOUGHT

I've got no pension or anything like that. I buy nice clothes and I live for today . . . . Maybe someday I'll regret it.

ON FACING LOSSES BY BEING
PREPARED TO LOSE EVEN MORE

If I suddenly lost everything, I

still think I could lose twenty
pounds and make a comeback.

ON WHAT A RETURN TO
COACHING WOULD ENTAIL

If I went back to coaching I would
have to take over. Nobody would
tell me who to play.

ON NEW LEVELS OF
INSINUATORY LOWS

A new low has been done by a
French paper here, I forget the
name of it. Yeah we won't say it
anyhow but I do forget it but anyhow, they insinuated that Burns
threw the game in Boston . . .
You can say a guy's a bad coach.
You can say a guy's this and that

but you don't say a guy's dishon-
est. It's a new low as far as I never
heard that . . .

ON THE RISK OF BEING THE
OBJECT OF SO MUCH SCRUTINY
WHILE LISTENING TO
THE CAR RADIO

I think that a lot of people think
that what I do on television is sort
of a put-on but that's the way I
am. I was listening to CBC one
time. They said that anybody
who is that aggressive, meaning
me, and who dresses that way is
a latent homosexual. They had
letters from psychiatrists saying
things like that. It's sure nice

driving along the highway and
hearing stuff like that.

ON ONE OF THE MANY WAYS
THAT BLUE
SERVES AS AN EXAMPLE

She was tough and that's how I
wanted the team. If they never
looked for a fight but once the
fight started, try to finish it and if
they were always strong and cou-
rageous, they'd be on my team.

ON WHAT BLUE SIGNIFIES

When I compared one of my
players to Blue it was like nomi-
nating him for knighthood.

ON WHY COACHES LIKE THEIR CANINE FRIENDS

No dumb questions, no criticisms, a dog just wants to be with you and love you.

ON WHAT SUBJECTS ARE TOO DELICATE EVEN FOR BLUE TO GET INTO MUCH

Blue and I never talk about international hockey as much as we can.

ON THE PRICE OF HAVING PRINCIPLES AND LOVING ONE'S CANINE COMPANION

I'm the only guy in the world who turned down fifteen thou-

sand dollars because my dog
wouldn't fly.

ON WHAT ELSE
TO LOVE

I love it when the CBCers, the left
wingers and the intellectuals go
nuts; I revel in it . . . . My way of
thinking has never gone above
that of a 36-year-old hockey
player.

ON BUILDING CHARACTER OR
WHAT'S WRONG WITH
WIVES THESE DAYS

My wife travelled with me. I have
to laugh at the wives now, that
they complain they don't have
their individualism and all that

stuff and here, me and my wife travelled and we lived in some of the rottenest apartments you've ever seen in your life.

ON WHAT'S ALL BEHIND ONE NOW

Life on the buses, you know, it was tough. It was tough.

ON CANADIAN IMMIGRATION POLICY

Unemployment is up, welfare is up, and they're bringing refugees in?

ON PROTESTING
TOO MUCH

I have the mentality of a construction worker.

ON THE SIGNIFICANCE OF CERTAIN SARTORIAL AND EMOTIVE PROPENSITIES AMONG HOCKEY COACHES

The more I see coaches with their plaid jackets and their string ties, I just eat that up. Beautiful. The more they don't show emotion on the bench, the more their interviews are bad, I think it's better for me.

ON WHAT TO MAKE OF PEOPLE
WHO TURN AWAY FROM ONE,
AND WHAT TO DO ABOUT THEM

But I don't care. People who don't like me, that's fine; if I met them I wouldn't like them either. They'd just be a bunch of left-wing liberals. I go out of my way to antagonize them.

ON JOHN TONELLI AS
AN EPITOME

John Tonelli is my kind of player. He is the epitome of grinder and in the Canada Cup he was the best in the world. He has a good Canadian heart.

ON HAVING MADE IT
UNSCATHED THROUGH A
BUNCH OF PEACE MARCHERS

So I finally make it through. So it is a great day and I go to the game that night and Canadians are hollering "Don Cherry sucks"—a good Canadian, I pays my taxes, leave my money here and didn't cost them anything—and they cheer Pavel Bure, who has one good game in five so I figure next year he'll have 16 good games.

ON SETTING THE RECORD
STRAIGHT ABOUT THOSE
EUROPEAN PLAYERS

I'm not racist. I just believe in Canadians first. Some European players should be playing here, like if you said Mats Naslund shouldn't be playing here you have rocks in your head. But a lot of the time you get people coming over from European when Canadians would do just fine.

ON WHAT WAS SPECIAL ABOUT THE 1989 GREY CUP BETWEEN SASKATCHEWAN AND HAMILTON

The best thing about this game, there's no Russians or Swedes playing.

ON THE TREND TOWARD TAKING COSSACKS IN SIBERIA

It became a trendy thing in the

draft this year when the first two expansion teams grabbed Europeans . . . It was a sad thing to see that players who got over a hundred points in the the Canadian Hockey League got passed over when they were taking cossacks in Siberia for a lot of Canadian and American kids . . . Sorta sad to see it.

ON PITTSBURGH GOALIE TOM BARRASSO'S SOFT SPOT

He couldn't stop a beachball.

ON THOSE GOOD OLD DAYS IN BOSTON

I loved coaching the Bruins more

then Gretzky and Bossy loved
scoring goals.

ON THE 1990 WORLD
JUNIOR VICTORY
VERSUS
THE COD WARS

And how about that Norris kid
from Newfoundland is he something else? Way to go from the
Rock! I know they don't like to
call it the Rock but I still call it the
Rock anyway. He said, you know
what he said 'You steal our fish,
you steal our fishing, you for-
eigners but you can't steal our
gold.' Way to go!

ON GETTING THE NORRIS KID
TO SOLVE THE THE COD
FISHERY PROBLEM

I would like to be the commissioner of fisheries. I'll tell you no foreign boat would take one of our fish. That's what I'd like to do Norris, you've got the hockey straightened out! Straighten out those guys in the fish!

ON PLANNING AHEAD,
OR SORT OF NOT

I don't think of the future. I sort of live for today.

ON BEING ASKED QUESTIONS
ON TV WHILE
ONE'S MOTHER
IS WATCHING

If somebody said to me 'okay, you've got your pick to do anything in the world, you can have any job in the world I can't think of a better job for a guy who grew up his whole life in hockey, grew up in Canada, and with your mother and all your friends watching, having Dave Hodge and Ron Maclean ask you 'What do you think of this.'

ON THE PRICE OF ACTING THAT WAY (EVEN WHEN YOU'RE GETTING PAID PEANUTS)

If you act that way, you're going to make a lot of enemies. And if you're a sensitive person then you shouldn't be doin' what I'm doin'. You make a lot of enemies. Some of them are bitter enemies. That's fine with me. I had a lot of bitter enemies when I played making $4,500 a year.

ON THE IMPORTANCE OF NOT THINKING

The thing is I don't think. I react. Because I played hockey so long and coached so long. You don't really think in hockey, you react all the time.

ON HANGING IN THERE, NAUTICALLY SPEAKING

I don't jump ship because the boat's rocking a little.

ON THE RUMOURS ABOUT JOHN BROPHY DRIFTING IN FROM AFAR

We used to hear about this guy in the Eastern League. It was like you heard about King Kong off in the jungle somewhere.

ON WHY ONE OUGHT TO BE
CAREFUL AROUND LARRY
ROBINSON AT CERTAIN TIMES

The stupidest thing in the world when you play Montreal is to wake up Larry Robinson. I used to tell my players not to wake him up because, if you do, he'll kill you.

FURTHER THOUGHTS ON THE
PRICE OF ACTING THAT WAY

I feel that some day they're going to come to me and say 'Well, you've just gone too far.'

ON THE UNFAIR USE OF THE REPLAY IN RESPECT OF HOCKEY FIGHTS

You sonofabitch! I guess you're going to replay that one eh? I betcha you're going to replay that one because my guy got beat.

ON THE PRICE OF CHOOSING A LIFE, EVEN IF ONE GOES TOO FAR AS A TV PERSONALITY

And that'll be it, but that's the life I choose.

ON SARTORIALITY AS IDENTITY

My shirt is my style . . . clean and tight.

ON THE SECRET OF THE FEELING OF REALLY STIFF COLLARS

I have the collars made with triple thickness because I feel I look good in them.

ON STICKING TO ONE'S SARTORIAL PRINCIPLES

I never ever have them done in the hotel. I never send them out either. Rose [Mrs. Cherry] washes then and they are ironed by hand. I like a little starch in them but not much.

ON TURNING THE THINGS OF
THE PAST TO NEW USES
IN THE PRESENT

Sometimes I use my grandfather Thomas Mackenzie's cuff links. They have his initials on them. If someone asks me what T.M. stands for, I say 'Top Man.'

ON KNOWING AT LEAST ONE
THING ABOUT ONESELF

I always wear shirts with French cuffs.

ON KNOWING WHAT YOU WANT
FROM STIFF COLLARS WELL
ENOUGH TO TELL YOUR MOTHER

She never liked me in them. She said "They push your chin up

and make you look pompous." I
said "That's how I like to look,
Mom."

ON GETTING ONESELF A
MONIKER,
EVEN IF IT'S *GRAPES*

When I was playing in Springfield in the American League, one
of the owner's pets had all his
misconducts paid and I didn't get
mine paid and I says I just didn't
want to. I said, 'Ah you're just a
teacher's pet anyhow!' and he
says, 'Ah, that's just sour grapes!'

ON THERE MUST BE *SOMETHING*
WRONG WITH
THE LINDROS TRADE

I feel sorry for Hextall and Ricci
and the rest. They signed their
contracts for the American taxes
because . . . you can stretch your
payment over a period of time,
whereas in Canada you can't.
Down there (taxes) would be
about thirty percent but if you go
to Quebec, it will be about fifty-
five percent. I feel sorry for them
because you know here is a kid,
Ricci, a young kid twenty one
years old, drafted by Philadel-
phia and now he is playing in
Quebec.

ON THE DEEPER IMPLICATIONS OF PLAYING IN QUEBEC

It's going to be very tough, especially on a guy like Hextall, because he's got three kids. He's already made the statement he's scared to death of bringing his three kids to Quebec in a French only school. So I feel very sorry for them.

ON BEING MISTAKEN FOR THE FRIENDLY GIANT AT THE TORONTO AIRPORT

I'm surprised they recognized me without me my giraffe.

ON THE SAD TRUTH OF WHAT IT'S ALL STRICTLY ON ACCOUNT OF

Well, there's no doubt all the superstars, if you will, are playing in the United States. That's strictly on account of money and taxes.

ON THE BEST THINGS IN LIFE FROM A TO B, WITH PARTICULARS FOR B

The best thing is playing and the second best thing is coaching . . . As far as coaching, I don't think you can get any better than coaching Bobby Orr, Phil Esposito, Wayne Cashman, Gerry Cheevers.

ON WHAT TO SAY WHEN ROGER NEILSON TELLS ONE NOT TO DANGLE ONE'S PREPOSITIONS

Hey Roger, where's the men's room at, you asshole?

SOURCES

The Boys of Saturday Night, Scott Young,
    Macmillan: 1990

Calgary Herald

Calgary Sun

"Coaches Corner," CBC-TV

The Columbian

The Globe and Mail

Grapes: A Vintage View of Hockey, Cherry/
    Fischler, Prentice-Hall: 1982

Inside Hockey

Lions in Winter, Goyens/Turowetz, Pen-
    guin: 1987

Macleans

Maple Leaf Blues, William Houston,
    McClelland & Stewart: 1990

Montreal Gazette

Saskatoon Star-Phoenix

Satelite Entertainment Network

Sunday Star

Toronto Star

Vancouver Province

Vancouver Sun

Index

ALLAN SAFARIK is a poet and freelance writer, and editor of *Quotations from Chairman Ballard* and co-editor of *Quotations of the Great One: The Little Book of Wayne Gretzky*. He lives in White Rock, B.C.

DOLORES REIMER comments on hockey from Dundurn, Saskatchewan. She is co-editor of *Quotations on the Great One: The Little Book of Wayne Gretzky*.

LITTLE RED BOOKS
FROM ARSENAL PULP PRESS